HOW TO GROW CARE MANAGE AND USE OREGANO FOR PROFIT

Guide To Growing And Profiting From Oregano Learn The Art Of Successful Oregano Cultivation, Effective Plant Care, And Strategic Harvesting And More

LARRY NANCY

"How to Grow, Care, Manage, and Use Oregano for Profit" is an invaluable resource for both novice and experienced farmers, entrepreneurs, and enthusiasts seeking to delve into the world of oregano cultivation and utilization. The book is structured in a comprehensive approach, guiding readers through every aspect of oregano farming, from the introductory fundamentals to advanced topics that are critical for maximizing profits.

Chapter 1 introduces readers to the fundamentals of oregano, laying the groundwork for a comprehensive understanding of this versatile herb. Chapter 2 delves into the various varieties of oregano, providing insights into their distinct characteristics and assisting readers in making informed decisions based on their specific needs and goals.

Chapters 3 and 4 provide practical advice on how to start and maintain a successful oregano garden, while Chapter 5 emphasizes eco-friendly and efficient farming practices that benefit both the environment and the quality of the oregano produced.

Chapter 6 covers harvesting and drying, which are critical steps in the cultivation process, and the book provides detailed instructions to ensure the highest quality oregano yield.

Chapter 7 addresses the post-harvest stage, guiding readers on how to process and add value to their oregano products, allowing them to create unique market offerings.

Moving beyond the farm, Chapter 8 focuses on marketing and selling strategies, providing readers with the tools they need to establish a successful market presence. Chapter 9 covers financial management specific to oregano farming, ensuring that readers can maximize profits and sustain a viable business.

The final chapter, Chapter 10, broadens the scope by exploring the culinary and medicinal applications of oregano. This section not only enriches the reader's understanding of the herb, but also opens doors to diverse revenue streams, making the book a comprehensive guide for those looking to maximize oregano's potential in various industries.

In essence, "How to Grow, Care, Manage, and Use Oregano for Profit" goes beyond the boundaries of a typical farming guide, serving as a holistic manual that seamlessly integrates agricultural practices with business strategies, providing a blueprint for success in the thriving world of oregano cultivation and utilization.

CHAPTER ONE
OREGANO

Oregano, scientifically known as Organum vulgare, is a versatile herb that originated in the Mediterranean region and has a rich history that dates back to ancient civilizations. The Greeks and Romans valued oregano not only for its culinary appeal but also for its medicinal properties.

The herb found its way into traditional medicine, where it was believed to have various health benefits.

The Rich History Of Oregano

Oregano's historical significance is deeply rooted in ancient cultures. The Greeks referred to it as "joy of the mountains," emphasizing its prevalence in rocky terrains. In ancient Greece, oregano was associated with Aphrodite, the goddess of love, symbolizing happiness and well-being.

 The Romans embraced oregano for its culinary applications and later introduced it to other European regions.

Its journey continued as explorers and traders disseminated it across continent.

Importance And Applications Of Oregano

Oregano, a key ingredient in Mediterranean and Italian cuisines, has antimicrobial and antioxidant properties and is rich in essential oils such as carvacrol and thymol. In traditional medicine, it has been used to alleviate respiratory issues, digestive problems, and even as a topical remedy for skin conditions.

Market Trends & Opportunities

The market for oregano has seen a significant upswing in recent years, with growing consumer awareness of the herb's health benefits and its integration into diverse culinary traditions contributing to increased demand.

The trend towards natural and organic products has further propelled oregano's popularity. Opportunities abound for entrepreneurs looking to capitalize on this trend, whether through cultivating oregano or developing value-added products. The market

Sustainable cultivation practices can not only meet market demands but also contribute to the overall ecological balance. Additionally, the rise of online marketplaces provides a platform for small-scale producers to reach a broader audience.

Farmers can take advantage of the demand for high-quality, organic oregano to cater to health-conscious consumers.

In conclusion, the rich history, diverse uses, and current market trends position oregano as a valuable herb with multifaceted potential.

Entrepreneurs and farmers alike can leverage this opportunity by understanding the herb's cultural significance, exploring its various applications, and aligning their efforts with evolving market dynamics. Oregano's journey from ancient civilizations to modern kitchens reflects its enduring appeal and promises a flavorful future.

CHAPTER TWO
UNDERSTANDING OREGANO VARIETIES

Oregano, a versatile herb known for its aromatic leaves and culinary uses, presents a myriad of varieties, each with unique characteristics that cater to different preferences and purposes. Popular oregano varieties include Organum vulgare (Common Oregano), Organum onites (Greek Oregano), and Organum Majorana (Sweet Marjoram), among others. These varieties vary not only in flavor and aroma, but also in growth habits, disease resistance, and adaptability.

Picking the Appropriate Kind for Your Requirements:

Common oregano (Origanum vulgare) is often preferred for its robust flavor and adaptability to diverse growing conditions, making it a versatile choice for culinary and medicinal applications. Greek oregano (Origanum onites) is renowned for its intense flavor, particularly suitable for Mediterranean dishes. Sweet marjoram (Origanum majorant) has a mild

Factors To Think About Regarding Weather And Soil

Common oregano thrives in well-drained soil and is resilient to a wide range of temperatures, making it adaptable to various climates; Greek oregano, on the other hand, prefers a drier and warmer climate, reflecting its Mediterranean origins. Understanding and optimizing the environmental factors that influence oregano's growth is essential for successful cultivation.

Growing Oregano Successfully

Oregano can be propagated through seeds, cuttings, or division of mature plants, depending on time constraints, resource availability, and desired scalability. To cultivate oregano for profit, growers must implement effective growing practices that ensure a robust and healthy crop.

Quality seeds or seedlings are essential, and growers should consider factors such as seed viability, germination rates, and disease resistance.

Proper soil preparation is fundamental to oregano cultivation. A well-drained soil rich in organic matter promotes healthy root development and reduces the risk of waterlogged conditions, which can be detrimental to oregano plants. Mulching helps retain soil moisture, suppresses weeds, and regulates soil temperature, all of which contribute to plant health.

Drip irrigation or soaker hoses can effectively provide targeted moisture without excessively wetting the foliage, but it is important to water oregano on a regular basis, especially during dry periods, because overwatering can cause root rot.

Managing Pests And Diseases

Oregano, like any other crop, is vulnerable to a variety of pests and diseases that can reduce yield and quality. To mitigate these risks while minimizing the use of chemical pesticides, Integrated Pest Management (IPM) strategies should be used. Aphids, spider mites, and whiteflies are common pests that affect oregano and can be controlled by introducing beneficial insects like ladybugs or predatory mites.

Crop rotation, selecting disease-resistant varieties, and maintaining proper spacing between plants are additional ways to prevent the onset and spread of fungal diseases like powdery mildew and root rot. Proper sanitation practices, such as the removal of infected plant material and the application of fungicides when necessary, can help prevent the onset and spread of these diseases.

Collecting Fruits And Overseeing Their Storage

Harvesting oregano is best done when the plants have reached a sufficient height and just before flowering, as this is when the essential oil content is at its highest. Using clean, sharp tools minimizes damage to the plants and allows for more efficient harvesting.

Post-harvest management entails drying the oregano to preserve its flavor and aroma.

 Proper drying methods, such as air-drying in a well-ventilated area or using a dehydrator, ensure the retention of essential oils. After drying, the leaves can be stored in airtight containers away from direct sunlight. Additionally, value-added products, such as oregano oil or dried blends, can increase the profitability of the venture.

Market Considerations And Value Addition

To successfully cultivate oregano for profit, growers must first understand market dynamics and consumer preferences. By conducting market research to identify potential buyers, such as restaurants, local markets, or health food stores, growers can tailor their cultivation practices to meet specific demands.

Adding value to oregano products through processing, packaging, and branding can increase marketability.

Establishing a strong online and offline presence, engaging in promotional activities, and obtaining necessary certifications for organic or sustainable practices can further differentiate oregano products in the market. Collaboration with local chefs, culinary experts, or health professionals can also provide insights into product development and marketing strategies, contributing to the overall success of the oregano cultivation venture.

In conclusion, the profitable cultivation of oregano requires a comprehensive understanding of the diverse varieties available, careful consideration of environmental factors, and the implementation of effective growing, pest management, and post-harvest practices. By aligning cultivation methods with market demands and incorporating value-added strategies, growers can not only yield a bountiful harvest, but also establish a sustainable and profitable oregano business.

CHAPTER THREE
SETTING UP YOUR OREGANO GARDEN

A successful oregano garden necessitates careful consideration of a variety of factors, beginning with the selection of an ideal location, which has a significant impact on the overall health and productivity of the oregano plants. Ideally, oregano thrives in areas with well-drained soil that receives ample sunlight throughout the day. It is critical to ensure that the soil is not waterlogged, as oregano plants are susceptible to

Oregano plants prefer well-drained, slightly alkaline soil with a pH ranging from 6.0 to 7.0.

A soil test before planting allows for accurate assessment and subsequent adjustments to meet the specific needs of oregano cultivation. Adding organic matter to the soil, such as compost or well-rotted manure, enhances its fertility and structure. Additionally,

Planting techniques play a pivotal role in achieving optimal growth and productivity in an oregano garden. It is advisable to start oregano from either seeds or cuttings, with each method having its own set of considerations. When planting from seeds, it is essential to sow them indoors in a seed tray before the last frost date, providing a warm and controlled environment for germination. Transplanting the seedlings into the garden should be done when the threat of frost has passed, ensuring that the soil has warmed up sufficiently. On the other hand, propagating oregano from cuttings involves snipping healthy stems from established plants and rooting them in a well-prepared soil bed. Regardless of the method chosen, maintaining adequate spacing between plants is crucial to allow for proper air circulation and prevent overcrowding. Watering the newly planted oregano and providing a layer of mulch aids in retaining soil moisture and suppressing weed growth. These planting techniques contribute significantly to the establishment of robust oregano plants poised for vigorous growth.

Care For Your Oregano Garden

To keep an oregano garden healthy and productive, it is essential to establish a regular watering schedule, especially during dry periods, to keep the soil evenly moist. Understanding the watering requirements is critical in preventing water-related issues like root rot.

Oregano is not particularly demanding in terms of fertilizer, but providing a balanced, all-purpose fertilizer during the growing season promotes healthy foliage and abundant herb production. It is recommended to apply fertilizer sparingly, as excessive nitrogen can lead to excessive leaf growth at the expense of flavor concentration in the leaves. Fertilization practices play a significant role in maintaining the nutrient levels necessary for robust oregano growth.

Pruning and harvesting guidelines are critical aspects of oregano care, contributing to the longevity and quality of the plants. Regular pruning helps maintain the desired shape of the oregano plants, prevents them from becoming overly leggy, and encourages bushier growth. Pruning can be done by snipping the tips of the stems, removing any dead or yellowing leaves, and thinning out overcrowded growth.

Harvesting should begin when the oregano plants reach a height of

Managing Pest And Disease Issues

Aphids, spider mites, and whiteflies are some of the most common pests that can infest oregano plants. Aphids feed on the sap of the plants, causing distorted growth and the transmission of viruses. Spider mites, tiny arachnids, can cause stippling and webbin

Powdery mildew, a common fungal disease that causes a white powdery substance on the leaves and affects the plant's overall health, can be prevented by spacing the plants properly, ensuring good air circulation, and avoiding overhead watering.

 If the disease does occur, applying fungicidal sprays or neem oil can help.

Using Oregano For Profit

Strategic marketing, the creation of value-added products, and the establishment of strong relationships with buyers are all necessary for harnessing the economic potential of oregano. Marketing strategies play a crucial role in creating awareness and demand for oregano products. Using online platforms, farmers' markets, and local grocery stores can help reach a larger audience. Highlighting the unique flavor profile and culinary versatility of oregano can attract consumers interested.

Creating value-added products, such as oregano-infused oils, vinegars, or packaged herb blends, can broaden the market for fresh or dried oregano leaves. Developing a brand identity and attractive packaging adds value to the products, making them more appealing to consumers. Providing clear information about cultivation practices, organic nature, or unique cha

Building and maintaining relationships with buyers is essential for sustained success in the oregano business. Establishing connections with local chefs, restaurants, and food businesses can lead to consistent and bulk sales. Offering samples, collaborating on recipe development, and providing reliable and timely deliveries contribute to building trust with buyers. Additionally, participating in local food events, festivals, and networking with other herb producers can open

To summarize, successfully growing, caring for, managing, and utilizing oregano for profit requires a comprehensive approach that encompasses site selection, soil preparation, planting techniques, watering, fertilization, pruning, harvesting, pest and disease management, marketing, value-added products, and buyer relationships. By understanding and implementing these concepts, individuals can establish and maintain a thriving oregano garden with the potential for a pro

CHAPTER FOUR
OREGANO CARE AND MAINTENANCE

Oregano (Origanum vulgare) is a versatile plant with aromatic leaves that are often used in culinary applications. Understanding efficient care and maintenance procedures is critical for ensuring successful production and maximizing profit yield.

<u>Watering strategies for oregano:</u>

Watering is a critical aspect of oregano cultivation because it directly influences plant health and productivity. Oregano prefers well-drained soil, and overwatering should be avoided to prevent root rot. It is essential to establish a consistent watering schedule, ensuring that the soil remains consistently moist but not waterlogged. Watering oregano more frequently may be necessary during hot and dry spells. Additionally, using drip irrigation or soaker hoses can be beneficial.

<u>Fertilization Practices:</u>

Oregano thrives in nutrient-rich soil, so a balanced, slow-release fertilizer with equal parts nitrogen, phosphorus, and potassium can promote healthy foliage, strong root development, and robust flavor. Fertilizer should be applied in early spring, before the growing season, and again in mid-summer to support continuous growth. Organic fertilizers, such as

<u>Pruning and Harvesting Tips:</u>

The best time to harvest oregano is when it reaches its peak flavor, which is usually just before

<u>Pest and Disease Management:</u>

Oregano is generally resistant to pests and diseases, but proactive management is crucial to prevent potential issues. Aphids, spider mites, and whiteflies are some of the most common pests that can harm oregano plants. Regularly inspecting the plants for any signs of infestation and using natural predators, such as ladybugs, or introducing beneficial insects like predatory mites, can help control pest populations.

You can also find effective organic alternatives, such as neem oil or insecticidal soap.

In conclusion, successful oregano cultivation for profit requires a holistic approach to care and maintenance. Implementing appropriate watering strategies, fertilization practices, and adopting effective pruning and harvesting techniques contribute to robust plant growth and flavor development. Vigilant pest and disease management is also necessary to safeguard the crop and ensure a sustainable and profitable oregano cultivation venture.

CHAPTER FIVE
SUSTAINABLE OREGANO FARMING PRACTICES

Organic Oregano Farming

Organic oregano farming involves cultivating oregano without the use of synthetic fertilizers, pesticides, or genetically modified organisms.

This method focuses on maintaining soil health and promoting biodiversity by using organic matter such as compost and well-rotted manure. Crop rotation is also an essential aspect of organic oregano farming, preventing soil-borne diseases and enhancing nutrient availability. Organ

Environmentally Friendly Pest Control Methods

To maintain the ecological balance of the farm and minimize the negative impact on beneficial insects, eco-friendly pest control methods are crucial in sustainable oregano farming.

Integrated Pest Management (IPM), which incorporates natural predators, companion planting, and crop rotation to control pests, is a key strategy. Beneficial insects like ladybugs and predatory beetles are introduced to the farm to prey on harmful pests, reducing the need for chemical pesticides.

Water Conservation Strategies

Water conservation is a critical aspect of sustainable oregano farming, especially in regions prone to water scarcity. Drip irrigation systems are commonly used to deliver precise amounts of water directly to the plant roots, minimizing water waste. Mulching around oregano plants helps retain soil moisture, reducing the frequency of irrigation needed. Additionally, rainwater harvesting systems can be implemented to capture and store rainwater for later use in irrigation.

Prudent Harvesting Techniques:

To maintain the plant's vitality, only a portion of the plant should be harvested at a time, leaving enough for regrowth. Harvesting oregano requires strategic planning to ensure optimal flavor and aroma retention. The best time to harvest oregano is during the flowering stage, as this is when essential oil concentrations are highest. Harvesting should be done in the morning, when the oil content is at its peak.

Careful Drying and Processing:

To preserve the flavor, aroma, and medicinal properties of oregano, it must be carefully dried and processed after harvesting. Drying can be done in small bundles, hanging them in a well-ventilated, shaded area, and avoiding direct sunlight, which can cause the loss of essential oils. Once dried, oregano leaves can be separated from the stems and stored in airtight containers to prevent moisture absorption.

Market Considerations and Value-Added Products.

<u>Understanding market trends:</u>

For profitable oregano farming, farmers should conduct market research to identify potential buyers and understand the demand for oregano products. This research can guide decisions related to cultivation practices, packaging, and pricing. Additionally, staying informed about culinary trends and health-conscious consumer preferences can help farmers tailor their production to meet market demand.

<u>Diversification with Value-Added Products:</u>

To maximize profits, oregano farmers can explore value-added products beyond the traditional dried herb market, such as producing oregano essential oil, infused oils, or dried herb blends for culinary or medicinal use.

By developing value-added products, farmers can differentiate their offerings and capture a larger share of the market.

Proper labeling and marketing strategies are crucial to highlight the unique qualities of these products and attract discernment.

Efficient Management And Record-Keeping

<u>Optimizing farm operations:</u>

Efficient management of oregano farms is essential for maximizing productivity and profitability. This includes strategic planning of planting schedules, crop rotation, and pest control measures. Farmers should also invest in quality seeds, equipment, and irrigation systems to ensure optimal crop growth. Regular monitoring of soil health, weather conditions, and plant health is required to make informed decisions and address issues promptly.

<u>Detailed Record Keeping:</u>

Accurate record-keeping is a fundamental aspect of successful oregano farming for profit. Farmers should maintain detailed records of expenses, yields, and sales. This information is crucial for financial planning, identifying cost-effective practices, and assessing the overall profitability of the venture. Record-keeping also aids in compliance with organic or certification standards, providing evidence of sustainable farming practices. Using digital tools or far

In conclusion, successful oregano farming for profit requires a comprehensive approach that includes sustainable farming practices, prudent harvesting and post-harvesting techniques, market considerations, value-added products, and efficient management with detailed record-keeping. By adopting organic farming methods, eco-friendly pest control measures, and water conservation strategies, oregano farmers can contribute to environmental sustainability while producing

CHAPTER SIX
HARVESTING AND DRYING OREGANO

Harvesting and drying oregano are critical stages in the cultivation process that significantly impact the herb's quality, flavor, and shelf life.

This section will delve into the intricate details of determining the right time to harvest, proper harvesting techniques, and effective drying methods for optimal flavor and extended shelf life.

Harvesting oregano at the right time is crucial for obtaining the best flavor and medicinal properties. Oregano plants are typically ready for harvest when they reach their peak oil content, which usually occurs just before the flowering stage. Monitoring the development of the herb is essential, and growers should pay close attention to the appearance of buds and the overall health of the plant. It is recommended to harvest oregano in the morning when the essential

Harvesting oregano should be done selectively and with sharp, clean scissors or pruning shears to avoid unnecessary damage to the plant.

Cutting the stems just above the leaf nodes promotes bushier growth and the plant's vitality.

To preserve the flavor and medicinal properties of oregano while extending its shelf life, one of the most traditional and effective methods is air drying. Bunches of oregano can be tied together and hung upside down in a well-ventilated area away from direct sunlight. Proper air circulation is crucial to prevent mold and mildew development. Oregano can also be dried using a food dehydrator set to a low temperature.

Microwave drying is a faster option, but it is not recommended for large quantities because it can result in uneven drying and loss of the herb's flavor and potency. To achieve uniform drying, the oregano should be spread evenly on a tray and set to the lowest temperature possible.

the process of harvesting and drying oregano requires careful consideration of various factors to ensure the highest quality and commercial viability of the herb.

From determining the right time to harvest to employing proper harvesting techniques and selecting appropriate drying methods, each step plays a critical role in the overall success of oregano cultivation for profit. By mastering these aspects, growers can optimize flavor, extend shelf life, and

CHAPTER SEVEN
OREGANO PROCESSING AND VALUE ADDITION

1. Post-harvest handling:

After harvesting oregano, proper handling techniques are necessary to preserve its flavor, aroma, and medicinal properties. Harvesting oregano in the morning, when the essential oil content is at its peak, ensures a higher quality yield.

After harvesting, oregano should be thoroughly cleaned to remove any dirt or debris. Sorting and grading are critical steps in post-harvest handling, ensuring that only the best-quality leaves and stems are chosen for further processing.

Proper packaging is also necessary to prevent damage during transportation and storage, and the packaging materials should be breathable to avoid moisture buildup, which can lead to mold growth.

2. Processing Oregano for Various Products:

Oregano can be processed in a variety of ways, including dried leaves, essential oils, and extracts. The dried leaves can be air-dried or dehydrated to remove moisture from them, and the powdered leaves can then be used in cooking.

Oregano extracts, which are high in antioxidants and other bioactive compounds, can be used to make herbal supplements, skincare products, and natural remedies. Steam distillation is a popular method for extracting oregano essential oil, which can then be marketed for its aromatic qualities and medicinal benefits.

Innovative processing techniques, such as freeze-drying, can also be explored to retain the maximum flavor and nutritional content of oregano. This diversification of product forms allows growers to cater to a larger market and capitalize on oregano's versatile applications in a variety of industries.

3. Adding Value to Your Oregano Products:

Adding value to oregano products is a critical aspect of maximizing profitability. Value addition involves transforming raw oregano into products that offer additional benefits or convenience to consumers. Branding and packaging are two effective ways. Creative and attractive packaging not only enhances shelf appeal but also communicates the product's quality and uniqueness.

Blending oregano with other complementary herbs and spices is another way to add value, resulting in unique seasoning mixes tailored for specific culinary applications. Marketing these blends as specialty products can attract a niche market interested in gourmet and exotic flavors.

Oregano-infused oils, sauces, or ready-to-use marinades, for example, can cater to the growing demand for convenient and flavorful cooking solutions. Investing in research and development to develop oregano-based products with enhanced functionality can also set your brand apart. Marketing materials emphasizing oregano's health benefits can also appeal to health-conscious customers.

Collaborations with chefs, nutritionists, and food scientists can bring fresh perspectives to product development, ensuring that oregano products not only taste great but also meet evolving consumer preferences. Exploring export opportunities for value-added oregano products can open up new markets and increase overall revenue for oregano growers. Overall, strategic value addition plays a pivotal role in establishing oregano as a premium and sought-after product.

CHAPTER EIGHT
MARKETING AND SELLING YOUR OREGANO PRODUCTS

Finding Your Ideal Customer Base

Identifying the target market for oregano cultivation and commercialization is critical to the venture's success. Understanding the demographics, preferences, and needs of potential consumers is essential for tailoring your product and marketing strategies. Conducting market research to analyze consumer behavior, trends, and competition will assist in pinpointing the target audience.

Branding And Packaging Strategy

To successfully market oregano products, it is essential to establish a strong brand identity and use effective packaging strategies. This includes selecting an appealing brand name, designing a memorable logo, and crafting a compelling brand story.

Consistent branding across various platforms fosters brand recognition and consumer trust.

Sales Channels And Distribution Options

Choosing the right sales channels and distribution options is pivotal in reaching a broader market and maximizing profitability. Oregano products can be distributed through various channels, including traditional retail outlets, farmers' markets, specialty stores, and online platforms.

Each channel has its advantages and challenges, and a strategic mix can be adopted for optimal market penetration. Collaborating with established retailers or wholesalers can enhance visibility and accessibility. Online platforms offer a global reach, allowing you to tap into a wider customer base. Additionally, direct-to-consumer sales through your website or local farm stands provide a more personal connection with customers. Efficient distribution logistics, including proper packaging and timely delivery, are critical for maintaining product quality and customer satisfaction. Regularly reassessing and adjusting your distribution strategy based on market trends and consumer preferences will contribute to long-term success in the competitive oregano market.

Growing Oregano: Cultivation And Management

<u>Cultivation Practices:</u>

Oregano thrives in well-drained soil with a slightly alkaline pH and requires 6-8 hours of sunlight per day for optimal growth. Proper spacing between plants, typically 12-18 inches, ensures good air circulation and prevents diseases. Regular irrigation is essential, but overwatering should be avoided to prevent root rot. As an additional measure, mulch the area surrounding the plants.

<u>Soil and nutrient management:</u>

Oregano thrives in well-drained, sandy-loam soil that has been enriched with organic matter. Adding compost or well-rotted manure before planting improves soil structure and fertility, and balanced fertilization with a focus on nitrogen, phosphorus, and potassium is essential for vigorous growth and maximum yield. Soil tests to assess nutrient levels and pH are recommended for appropriate amendments.

<u>Pest and Disease Control:</u>

Oregano is generally resistant to pests and diseases, but preventive measures are essential to ensure a healthy crop. Implementing companion planting with insect-repelling herbs like basil and marigold can deter pests. Regular inspection of plants for signs of pests, such as aphids or spider mites, allows for early intervention. Organic pest control methods, such as neem oil or insecticidal soap, are preferable to reduce chemical residues in the final product.

<u>Harvesting and Postharvest Management:</u>

Proper drying methods, such as hanging bunches in a well-ventilated area or using a dehydrator, are essential for preserving the quality of oregano.

The best time to harvest oregano is just before the plant flowers, usually in the morning, when the essential oil concentration is at its peak.

Using Oregano For Profit: Culinary And Medical Applications

<u>Culinary applications:</u>

Oregano is a versatile herb that can be used in a variety of dishes, including marinades, soups, and grilled meats, making it a popular herb in the food industry. It is a key ingredient in Mediterranean and Italian cuisines, where it adds a robust and savory flavor to pasta sauces, pizzas, and salads. Oregano's compatibility with other cuisines, such as Mexican and Middle Eastern, broadens its market appeal.

<u>Medical Applications:</u>

Oregano's essential oils, particularly carvacrol and thymol, have antimicrobial and antioxidant properties, making it a potential ingredient in natural remedies for respiratory issues, digestive problems, and immune support. Extracts of oregano are used in supplements, herbal teas, and topical products. Developing and doing research in tandem Product innovation and diversification:

To maximize profit from oregano cultivation, exploring product innovation and diversification is key. Beyond dried oregano leaves, consider developing value-added products such as oregano-infused oils, seasoning blends, or herbal teas. Packaging these products creatively and emphasizing their unique selling points can cater to different consumer preferences.

CHAPTER NINE
FINANCIAL MANAGEMENT IN OREGANO FARMING
Cost Analysis And Budgeting

A comprehensive cost analysis involves identifying and evaluating all expenses associated with the cultivation, care, and harvest of oregano, including costs for seeds or seedlings, soil amendments, fertilizers, pesticides, labor, equipment, and irrigation. A detailed budget assists farmer in allocating resources efficiently and planning for potential challenges.

Pricing strategies:

In order to maximize profits in the oregano farming business, farmers must develop effective pricing strategies that take into account market demand, competitor pricing, and the quality of their oregano products. Understanding the production costs identified through cost analysis is crucial in setting prices that cover expenses and generate a profit.

Farmers can use various pricing models, such as cost-plus pricing or market-oriented pricing.

Record-keeping for Profitability:

Maintaining meticulous records is a fundamental aspect of effective financial management in oregano farming. Accurate record-keeping allows farmers to track expenses, revenue, and overall financial performance, which is invaluable for making informed decisions, identifying areas for cost savings, and optimizing resource allocation.

Care and management of oregano plants:

Preparing the soil and choosing the location

Oregano grows on well-drained soil with a pH range of slightly alkaline to neutral. Before planting, the soil should be tested for composition and fertility, and soil amendments may be required to improve drainage or adjust pH levels.

Proper soil preparation, including plowing and tilling, creates

Planting and Propagation:

Oregano can be propagated through seeds, cuttings, or division, depending on the farmer's goals and resources. Seeds can be started indoors and transplanted once seedlings are established, whereas cuttings provide a faster method of propagation. Proper planting practices, such as spacing and

Cultivation Practices:

To maintain healthy oregano plants and maximize yields, effective cultivation practices are essential. Watering oregano plants on a regular basis, especially during dry periods, is necessary for optimal growth. Mulching around the plants helps retain moisture, suppress weeds, and regulate soil temperature.

Pruning is another important aspect of cultivation, as it encourages bushier growth and increases the concentration of essential oils responsible for flavor and aroma.

<u>Harvest and Post-Harvest Handling:</u>

Harvesting oregano at the right time is critical for obtaining the best flavor and aroma.

The optimal time for harvesting is typically when the plant has reached full maturity but before flowering occurs. Harvesting should be done in the morning when essential oil concentrations are highest. After harvesting, oregano should be handled carefully to avoid bruising or damaging the leaves.

Post-harvest processing may include drying the leaves for culinary use or extracting

<u>Utilization and Value-Added Products:</u>

In addition to traditional culinary uses, oregano farmers can explore value-added products to diversify their income streams. Processing oregano into dried herbs, spice blends, or essential oils allows farmers to tap into different markets and cater to a broader range of consumers.

Developing unique and high-quality products can differentiate a farmer's brand and create a competitive edge in the market.

Collaborating with local chefs, restaurants, or specialty food producers

<u>Market analysis and marketing strategy:</u>

In order to understand consumer preferences, market trends, and potential competitors in the oregano industry, farmers must conduct thorough market research, identify target markets, assess demand, and tailor their products to meet consumer expectations.

Effective marketing strategies include developing a strong brand identity, utilizing digital and traditional marketing channels, and engaging with the target audience through promotions and events.

Risk Management and Sustainability Practices:

Organic farming, water conservation, and biodiversity enhancement are some of the sustainable practices that oregano farmers can use to reduce their environmental impact and build long-term resilience.

 Diversifying crops or income streams can also serve as a risk-mitigation strategy. Farmers should stay up to date on industry trends and regulatory changes.

CHAPTER TEN
EXPLORING THE CULINARY AND MEDICINAL USES OF OREGANO

Oregano, a versatile herb known for its aromatic and flavorful leaves, has gained widespread attention for its diverse applications in both culinary and medicinal realms. In the culinary sphere, oregano finds its place in an array of dishes, enhancing the flavor profile of various cuisines. Oregano, rich in essential oils such as carvacrol and thymol, imparts a distinctive taste to dishes like pasta sauces, pizzas, and grilled meats.

Oregano's essential oils have been studied for their potential in combating bacterial and fungal infections, making it a natural remedy for a variety of ailments. Oregano has been traditionally used to address a wide range of health concerns, from respiratory issues to digestive disorders, and it is important to investigate these medicinal properties.

Creative Oregano-Based Products

Oregano's aromatic properties make it an ideal candidate for use in a variety of products, including oils, vinegars, and condiments, which have grown in popularity due to their distinct flavors and health benefits. Creating these products necessitates knowledge of extraction methods, blending techniques, and proper packaging to ensure product stability and longevity.

CONCLUSION

To cultivate oregano for profit, a comprehensive approach to growth, care, management, and utilization is required. This includes selecting the right variety, understanding soil and environmental requirements, and implementing sustainable farming practices. Proper irrigation, pest control, and pruning are necessary to ensure a robust and healthy crop.

Strategic harvesting is also part of effective management.

To capitalize on the commercial potential of oregano, one must delve into its diverse applications. Integrating oregano into culinary delights requires a keen understanding of flavor pairing, cooking techniques, and consumer preferences. Exploring the medicinal benefits involves a careful examination of its bioactive compounds, potential therapeutic uses, and adherence to regulatory guidelines. Additionally, venturing into creative oregano-based products requires innovation.

To cultivate and use oregano profitably, farmers and entrepreneurs must keep up with market demands, consumer trends, and scientific advancements. In essence, the journey from seed to market-ready product involves a blend of agricultural expertise, culinary finesse, and business acumen. By embracing these concepts, one can not only cultivate a thriving ore.